Burgers
'n
Fries
'n
Cinnamon Buns

Low-fat, meatless versions
of fast food favorites

Bobbie Hinman

THE BOOK PUBLISHING COMPANY
SUMMERTOWN, TENNESSEE

© 1993 by Bobbie Hinman
Cover design: Nava Atlas

Published in the United States by
Book Publishing Company
P.O. Box 99
Summertown, TN 38483
888-260-8458   bookpubl@usit.net
http://bpc.thefarm.org

02 01 00 99 98   3 4 5 6 7

ISBN 0-913990-16-7

For information on how to arrange an appearance by the
author for your hospital or organization, contact the Book
Publishing Company at 931-964-3571.

Hinman, Bobbie.
    Burgers 'n fries 'n cinnamon buns : low-fat, meatless
versions of fast food favorites / Bobbie Hinman. - Rev. ed.
            p.   cm.
    Includes index
    ISBN 0-913990-16-7
    1. Low-fat diet-Recipes. 2. Low-calories diet-Recipes.
3.vegetarian cookery. 4. Junk food.   I. Title
RM237.7.H555   1993
641,5'638-dc20   93-26027
                                          CIP

Table of Contents

Nutritional Information

The recipe analysis for this book was done with the Nutripak Professional Plus System (Nutrient Data Resources, Cleveland, Ohio).

Optional ingredients are not included in the calculations. When there is a choice of two ingredients, the analysis is based on the first one mentioned. The nutritional analysis may vary slightly depending on the brands of food that are used. If a recipe contains a "trace of a particular item (less than ½ gram of protein, fat, or carbohydrate, or less than ½ milligram of sodium or cholesterol), the number will be listed as zero. In recipes that call for salt "to taste," the salt has not been included in the analysis.

ABOUT THE AUTHOR

BOBBIE HINMAN

Bobbie Hinman has been a pioneer in the field of low-fat cooking. When she first discovered, over 20 years ago, that her family had a hereditary cholesterol problem, she was a "typical high-fat gourmet cook." Determined to raise her family on a healthy low-fat diet, and aware of the fact that there were few, if any, teaching cookbooks available at the time, Bobbie set out to find ways to make healthy meals that were also tasty meals. She describes her transition to a vegetarian diet as a "natural progression" in her quest to master the art of healthy cooking and, at the same time, provide delicious meals for herself and her family.

Bobbie is constantly in demand as a speaker and cooking teacher and has been a guest on numerous television and radio shows. She recently completed a media tour for General Mills where she discussed the benefits of eating a low-fat, high-fiber diet. Bobbie is the co-author of *Lean and Luscious and Meatless*, one of today's best-selling vegetarian cookbooks. In addition to writing cooking columns for several monthly publications, Bobbie is a frequent contributor to the *Vegetarian Journal*. She also travels extensively, teaching classes and speaking to hospital groups, cardiac centers, weight management centers, colleges, and private organizations.

Even with her busy schedule, Bobbie still finds time to read as many health publications as possible and consult with doctors, dietitians, and other health professionals. Her goal is to keep abreast of the latest advances in food and health issues so that she can continue to help people enjoy the benefits of healthful eating.

Bobbie resides in Delaware with her husband Harry. They have four grown children.

Foreword

Most of us know we should eat a diet low in fat and cholesterol. But what does that mean in terms of food choices? No more milkshakes, French fries, or pizza? Not if we choose foods like those in this book.

Bobbie Hinman has used a skillful blend of science and art to develop recipes for foods that taste good and are low in fat. These are healthy foods the whole family can enjoy. In addition, by choosing dishes like these and thereby eating lower on the food chain (and avoiding the excess packaging so common in fast food restaurants), we are doing our planet a favor.

Healthy food, fun food, and creative food! What more could we ask for?

Reed Mangels, Ph.D., R.D.
Nutrition Advisor,
The Vegetarian Resource Group

Introduction

This is a book to have fun with. It contains recipes for popular fast food favorites that you can now make at home. The recipes are easy to prepare and the calories and fat content have been greatly reduced, making these versions more healthful than the originals. The recipes are all meatless and egg-free, and contain only a small amount of dairy products, all of which can be substituted with soy-based (or other non-dairy) products if desired.

Lest people think that this book is advocating fast food, or even implying that those who prefer meatless meals probably feel deprived, remember, the purpose is purely enjoyment. And, let's face it, in today's fast-paced society, who doesn't welcome ideas for quick and easy meals?

So, have fun, eat healthfully, and, most of all....

Enjoy!!!

Silver Dollar Pancakes – small, fluffy pancakes, made either plain or with your choice of fruit or carob chips 10

Fruited French Toast – slices of whole wheat bread, dipped in a fruit pureé, then cooked until brown and crisp, and served with pure maple syrup 11

Scrambled Tofu – delicately spiced tofu, scrambled and heated through; can also be made with lightly browned onions and/or green peppers 12

Hash Browns – chopped potatoes and onions, lightly salted and cooked until crisp 13

Sausage and Biscuits – delicious bean and rice patties, seasoned with aromatic spices and served in a tender whole wheat biscuit 14

Biscuits and Gravy – tender whole wheat biscuits, smothered in a smooth bean gravy 16

Silver Dollar Pancakes

These small, fluffy pancakes can be enjoyed as is, or you can add your choice of carob chips or fruit. Some delicious additions are blueberries, banana chunks, raisins, or well-drained crushed pineapple.

Makes 4 servings
(8 pancakes per serving)

¾	cup whole wheat flour
½	cup all-purpose flour
2	teaspoons baking powder
2	tablespoons sugar
1½	cups skim milk or low-fat soymilk
1	tablespoon plus 1 teaspoon vegetable oil
1½	teaspoons vanilla extract

In a large bowl, sift together both types of flour, baking powder, and sugar.

In a small bowl, combine remaining ingredients. Add to dry mixture, mixing just until all ingredients are moistened. (Batter will be lumpy.)

Preheat a nonstick skillet or griddle over medium heat. Oil it lightly or spray with a nonstick cooking spray.

Drop batter onto hot griddle, using 1 tablespoon of batter for each pancake. Turn pancakes once, when tops are bubbly and edges are dry. Cook until golden brown on both sides. (Makes thirty-two 2½-inch pancakes.)

Each serving provides:			
229	Calories	38 g	Carbohydrate
8g	Protein	245 mg	Sodium
5g	Fat	2 mg	Cholesterol

Fruited French Toast

What a delectable, fruity breakfast treat—this unusual egg-free, dairy-free delicacy, drizzled with pure maple syrup!

Makes 2 servings

1	medium, ripe banana
½	cup orange juice
1	teaspoon vanilla extract
⅛	teaspoon ground cinnamon
4	slices whole wheat bread, preferably a few days old

In a blender container, combine banana, orange juice, vanilla, and cinnamon. Blend until smooth.

Pour mixture into a shallow baking pan or bowl.

Place bread in pan and turn gently several times until bread is completely saturated.

Preheat a nonstick griddle or skillet over medium heat. Oil it lightly or spray with a nonstick cooking spray.

Place bread on griddle and drizzle with any remaining banana mixture. Cook until toast is lightly browned on both sides, turning several times and adding nonstick spray if needed.

Each serving provides:			
221	Calories	43 g	Carbohydrate
7g	Protein	261 mg	Sodium
3g	Fat	0 mg	Cholesterol

Scrambled Tofu

Here's a quick and easy alternative to a popular egg dish. The use of turmeric, a delicately flavored spice, also adds a nice yellow color.

Makes 4 servings

1	pound medium or firm tofu, sliced, drained well between towels
¼	teaspoon garlic powder
¼	teaspoon turmeric
⅛	teaspoon pepper
	Salt to taste

Place tofu in a large bowl and mash with a fork. Add spices and mix well.

Heat a large nonstick skillet over medium heat. Place tofu in pan. Cook, stirring frequently, until hot.

Variations: Cook chopped onions and/or green pepper in skillet in 1 or 2 teaspoons of oil until nicely browned before adding tofu.

Each serving provides:			
89	Calories	2 g	Carbohydrate
9 g	Protein	8 mg	Sodium
6 g	Fat	0 mg	Cholesterol

Hash Browns

These all-time favorites have a minimum amount of oil and a maximum amount of flavor. They're great as a side dish with dinner, or as a perfect brunch dish alongside our Scrambled Tofu. (See index for recipe).

Makes 4 servings

1   tablespoon vegetable oil
4   cups cold, cooked potatoes, cut into ¼- to ½-inch cubes (If the potatoes have been baked, carefully remove the skins and use them to make the delicious Baked Potato Skins in the Deli Chapter. If the potatoes have been boiled, the skin is usually soft enough to leave on.)
1   cup finely chopped onions
      Salt, pepper, and paprika to taste

Heat oil in a large nonstick skillet over medium heat. Add potatoes and onions. Sprinkle with salt and pepper to taste and lots of paprika. Cook, stirring frequently, about 10 minutes, or until edges of potatoes are brown and crisp.

Variation: Add ½ cup finely chopped green pepper along with the onions and potatoes.

Each serving provides:

171	Calories	33	g	Carbohydrate	
3g	Protein	8	mg	Sodium	
4g	Fat	0	mg	Cholesterol	

Breakfast

NOW BEING SERVED

Sausage and Biscuits

These mock sausages can be frozen and then browned in no time. And the biscuits, of course, have many other delicious uses.

Sausage

Makes twelve 3-inch patties

1	1-pound can kidney beans, rinsed and drained (or 2 cups of cooked beans)
1	cup cooked brown rice
2	tablespoons ketchup
¼	teaspoon ground sage
⅛	teaspoon dried thyme
⅛	teaspoon ground savory
⅛	teaspoon garlic powder
¼	teaspoon salt
¼	teaspoon pepper
¼	teaspoon fennel seeds, crushed slightly (Roll between 2 layers of wax paper with a rolling pin.)

Place beans, rice, and ketchup in a large bowl. Sprinkle evenly with spices. Mash well with a fork or potato masher, making sure that spices are evenly distributed. (Rice will be lumpy.)

Divide chilled mixture into 12 portions. Roll each portion into a ball. Flatten each ball into a 3-inch patty.

Preheat a large nonstick skillet or griddle over medium heat. Oil lightly or spray with a nonstick cooking spray.

Cook sausages until brown on both sides, turning frequently to brown evenly. Oil or spray pan again if necessary.

Serve hot on biscuits. (Recipe follows).

Each sausage patty provides:			
56	Calories	11 g	Carbohydrate
3 g	Protein	217 mg	Sodium
0 g	Fat	0 mg	Cholesterol

Biscuits

Makes twelve 3-inch biscuits

1	cup whole wheat flour
1	cup all-purpose flour
1	tablespoon baking powder
½	teaspoon salt
3	tablespoons vegetable oil
1	cup skim milk or low-fat soymilk

Preheat oven to 450 °.

Lightly oil a baking sheet or spray with a nonstick cooking spray.

Into a large bowl, sift both types of flour, baking powder and salt. (Gently stir any bran that is left in the sifter back into the flour.)

Add oil. Mix with a fork or pastry blender until mixture resembles coarse crumbs.

Add milk. Stir until dry ingredients are moistened.

Place dough on a floured surface and knead a few times until dough holds together in a ball. (If dough is sticky, you may need to add a bit more flour.) Place a sheet of wax paper over dough and roll to ½-inch thickness. Carefully remove wax paper.

Using a 3-inch biscuit cutter or a glass, cut 12 biscuits. (Scraps can be put together and rolled again.)

Place biscuits on prepared baking sheet.

Bake 10 minutes, until bottoms of biscuits are lightly browned.

Remove to a wire rack and serve warm for best flavor.

(Leftovers can be reheated in a toaster or oven.)

Each biscuit provides:			
107	Calories	16 g	Carbohydrate
3 g	Protein	201 mg	Sodium
4 g	Fat	0 mg	Cholesterol

Biscuits and Gravy

Here's a perfect use for leftover biscuits. It's quick, easy, and healthful, too.
Use the biscuit recipe on the preceding page and add this unusual gravy.

Bean Gravy

Makes 4 servings
(½ cup each serving)

1	1-pound can Great Northern beans, rinsed and drained (or 2 cups of cooked beans)
1	teaspoon vegetable broth mix
1	tablespoon finely chopped onion
¾	cup water
⅛	teaspoon pepper
¹⁄₁₆	teaspoon garlic powder
½	cup nutritional yeast

In a blender container, combine all ingredients. Blend until smooth. Place in a small saucepan and heat until hot and bubbly.
Spoon over biscuits.

Each serving (gravy only) provides:

153	Calories	25	g	Carbohydrate
14 g	Protein	107 mg		Sodium
1 g	Fat	0 mg		Cholesterol

Tacos – a delicious mixture of bulgur, onions, green peppers, and kidney beans in a spicy tomato sauce; served in crisp taco shells with your choice of toppings 18

Taco Salad – our famous taco filling, served on a bed of tortilla chips and lettuce and topped with tomatoes, onions, olives, and your choice of low-fat Cheddar cheese or soy cheese 19

Burritos – tortillas filled with our own spicy bean mixture and served with your choice of hot or mild salsa 20

Tofu Fajitas – strips of tofu with sliced onions and green peppers, marinated in a delicate sauce, then stir-fried; served in a rolled flour tortilla 21

Vegetarian Chili – lots of vegetables and kidney beans, simmered in a thick tomato sauce and spiced just right 22

Hot Nacho Snacks – tortilla chips, topped with lettuce, tomatoes, green onions, olives, and your choice of low-fat Cheddar cheese or soy cheese; baked until the cheese is melted, and served with lots of salsa 23

Tacos

For toppings try chopped tomatoes, lettuce, onions, black olives, shredded soy cheese, and lots of salsa.

Makes 12 tacos

1	cup water
½	cup bulgur (cracked wheat)
2	teaspoons vegetable oil
½	cup chopped onions
½	cup chopped green pepper
1	8-ounce can salt-free (or regular) tomato sauce
1	1-pound can kidney beans, rinsed and drained (or 2 cups of cooked beans)
2	teaspoons chili powder
1	teaspoon ground cumin
¼	teaspoon garlic powder
⅛	teaspoon cayenne pepper
12	taco shells

Bring water to a boil in a small saucepan. Add bulgur. Cover, reduce heat to low, and simmer 15 minutes, until water has been absorbed.

Preheat oven to 350°.

While bulgur is cooking, heat oil in a large nonstick skillet over medium heat. Add onions and green pepper. Cook until tender, about 5 minutes.

Add tomato sauce, beans, spices, and cooked bulgur. Mix well, mashing beans with a fork. Cover, reduce heat to low, and cook 5 minutes.

Wrap taco shells in foil and, while filling is cooking, heat shells in oven for 5 minutes.

To serve, fill shells with bean mixture, then top with your choice of toppings.

Each taco (without toppings) provides:			
133	Calories	22 g	Carbohydrate
5 g	Protein	236 mg	Sodium
3 g	Fat	0 mg	Cholesterol

Taco Salad

All of the taco ingredients, piled high, make a filling meal-in-one. Kids (of all ages) will love this one!

Makes 6 servings

1	recipe Taco filling (See preceding page)
12	taco shells, broken into bite-size pieces (or one 7-ounce bag of baked tortilla chips)
4	cups shredded lettuce
2	cups chopped tomato
¾	cup chopped onions
¼	cup thinly sliced black or green olives
6	ounces shredded low-fat Cheddar cheese or soy cheese (1½ cups)
	Jar of mild or hot salsa

Prepare taco filling according to directions.

To serve, arrange broken taco shells (or tortilla chips) on each of 6 dinner plates. Divide lettuce evenly and place on shells. Then top with hot taco filling, tomato, onions, olives, cheese, and salsa.

Note: The nutritional analysis for this recipe was based on servings of ¼ cup of salsa. To reduce the amount of sodium, you can use smaller portions of salsa.

Each serving provides:	
413 Calories	62 g Carbohydrate
17g Protein	1711 mg Sodium
13 g Fat	12 mg Cholesterol

Burritos

Topped with lots of salsa, these burritos can't be beat. This recipe serves four as a great snack or two as a filling dinner.

Makes 4 servings

4	6-inch flour tortillas
2	teaspoons vegetable oil
1	cup chopped onions
2	cloves garlic, finely minced
1	1-pound can kidney beans, rinsed and drained (or 2 cups of cooked beans)
½	teaspoon dried oregano
½	teaspoon ground cumin
1	teaspoon chili powder
	Salt and pepper to taste
	Jar of mild or hot salsa

Preheat oven to 350 °.

Stack tortillas and wrap tightly in foil.

Heat in oven for 10 minutes. While tortillas are heating, prepare burrito filling:

Heat oil in a large nonstick skillet over medium heat. Add onions and garlic. Cook, stirring frequently, 5 minutes, or until onions start to brown.

Add beans to skillet. Sprinkle with spices. Mix well, mashing about half of the beans with a fork. Cook until beans are heated through.

Divide mixture evenly into the centers of the heated tortillas. Fold in tops and bottoms of tortillas, then fold in the sides so that filling is completely enclosed.

Serve right away or wrap in foil and place in oven to keep warm until serving time.

Serve with salsa.

Note: The nutritional analysis for this recipe was based on servings of ¼ cup of salsa. To reduce the amount of sodium, you can use smaller portions of salsa.

Each burrito provides:		
339 Calories		63 g Carbohydrate
13g Protein		1534 mg Sodium
6 g Fat		0 mg Cholesterol

Tofu Fajitas

From **Lean and Luscious and Meatless***, *these juicy fajitas can be served either plain or topped with salsa. Marinate the tofu and vegetables ahead of time and prepare the fajitas "in a flash" when you're ready.*

Makes 6 fajitas

1	pound firm tofu, cut into matchstick-size pieces
1½	cups onion, thinly sliced
1½	cups green pepper, thinly sliced
1	4-ounce can chopped green chilies
½	cup orange juice
1	tablespoon olive oil
2	tablespoons vinegar
3	cloves garlic, finely chopped
1	teaspoon ground cumin
1	teaspoon ground coriander
1	teaspoon dried oregano
6	6-inch flour tortillas

Place tofu, onions, and green pepper in a 9 x 13-inch baking pan.

In a small bowl, combine remaining ingredients, except tortillas, mixing well. Pour over tofu mixture.

Cover pan and refrigerate 4 or 5 hours, gently stirring tofu mixture occasionally.

To cook: Wrap tortillas tightly in aluminum foil and heat in a 350° oven for 10 minutes.

Heat a large nonstick skillet over medium-high heat. Drain tofu mixture (reserving marinade) and place in skillet. Cook, stirring gently, until vegetables are slightly tender. Add marinade, a little at a time, to keep mixture from sticking. (If you prefer a juicy fajita filling, add all of the marinade.)

To serve, spoon tofu filling into the center of heated tortillas, roll, and enjoy.

*Lean and Luscious and Meatless is a collection of 350 easy-to-prepare and delicious meat-free recipes by Bobbie Hinman and Millie Snyder. See order form in back of book.

Each fajita provides:			
238	Calories	24 g	Carbohydrate
15 g	Protein	269 mg	Sodium
11 g	Fat	0 mg	Cholesterol

Vegetarian Chili

Just add a chunk of crusty, whole grain bread and your meal is complete!

Makes 6 servings

2	teaspoons vegetable oil
3	cloves garlic, finely chopped
1	cup chopped onions
1	cup chopped green pepper
1	cup chopped celery
1	cup chopped carrots
2	cups sliced mushrooms
1	28-ounce can crushed tomatoes (in tomato pureé, if available)
2	8-ounce cans salt-free (or regular) tomato sauce
2	1-pound cans kidney beans, rinsed and drained (about 4 cups of cooked beans)
1	10-ounce package frozen corn
1	teaspoon dried oregano
1	teaspoon dried basil
1	teaspoon ground cumin
1	tablespoon chili powder (or more, according to taste)
	Salt to taste

Heat oil in a large saucepan over medium heat. Add garlic, onions, green pepper, celery, carrots, and mushrooms. Cook 5 minutes, stirring frequently.

Add remaining ingredients, mixing well. Bring mixture to a boil, then reduce heat to low, cover, and cook 1 hour, or until vegetables are tender. (For uniform cooking, chop all of the vegetables into similar sized pieces.)

To serve, divide chili into serving bowls and top with crushed crackers or a light sprinkling of low-fat Cheddar cheese or soy cheese.

Each serving provides:			
299	Calories	58 g	Carbohydrate
14 g	Protein	865 mg	Sodium
4 g	Fat	0 mg	Cholesterol

Hot Nacho Snacks

This crunchy "finger-food" treat is great for snacks or parties.

Makes 8 servings

1	large bag tortilla chips (Choose the ones that are baked, rather than fried. One large bag weighs approximately 7 ounces, depending on the brand.)
6	ounces shredded low-fat Cheddar cheese or soy cheese (1½ cups)
1	large tomato, chopped into ½-inch pieces
¼	cup thinly sliced black olives (or a combination of black olives and stuffed green olives)
2	tablespoons thinly sliced green onions
1	cup shredded lettuce
	Jar of mild or hot salsa

Preheat oven to 375°.

Spread tortilla chips evenly in an ungreased 10 x 15-inch shallow baking pan. Sprinkle with *half* of the cheese, followed by the tomato, olives, green onions, and then the remaining cheese.

Bake until cheese is melted, about 5 minutes.

Remove from oven and top with lettuce.

Serve by either giving each person a plate on which to pile chips and salsa for dipping, or spread salsa over the chips in the pan and dig in!

Each serving provides:			
128	Calories	16 g	Carbohydrate
7g	Protein	564 mg	Sodium
4 g	Fat	0 mg	Cholesterol

Beany Burgers – beans and rice, along with onions and spices, made into burgers and served on a whole grain bun with your choice of toppings 26

Almost French Fries – the finest baking potatoes, cut into thin strips and then baked until crisp **27**

Tofu Nuggets – nuggets of firm tofu, rolled in our combination of wheat germ and spices and baked until crisp; served with your choice of dipping sauces 28

Dipping Sauces – your choice of our famous sauces; choose from our peach flavored Sweet and Sour Sauce or our creamy Maple Mustard 29

Baked Potato Bar – top your own steamy baked potato with any (or all!) of our delicious toppings; choose from a wide variety of vegetables, sauces, and spices, along with many unusual surprises 30

Strawberry Milkshake – a thick, rich shake made from frozen berries that are lightly sweetened and blended with your choice of skim milk or low-fat soymilk 31

MENU

Beany Burgers

From **Lean and Luscious and Meatless***, *these moist burgers are delicious served on a bun with your favorite burger "fixins."*

Makes 8 burgers

1	1-pound can kidney beans, rinsed and drained (or 2 cups of cooked beans)
2	cups cooked brown rice
2	tablespoons ketchup
½	teaspoon garlic powder
1	teaspoon dried oregano
⅛	teaspoon dried thyme
¼	teaspoon ground sage
	Salt and pepper to taste
¼	cup very finely chopped onions

In a large bowl, combine beans, rice, ketchup, and spices. Mash with a fork or a potato masher until beans are mashed well. (Rice will be lumpy.)

Add chopped onions and mix well.

Divide mixture evenly and form into 8 burgers, ½ to ¾-inch thick. Wet your hands slightly to avoid sticking.

Lightly oil a nonstick griddle or skillet, or spray with a nonstick cooking spray. Preheat over medium heat. Place burgers on griddle and cook until browned on both sides, turning burgers several times.

Serve hot with lettuce, tomato, relish, ketchup, or your favorite burger toppings.

"Lean and Luscious and Meatless is a collection of 350 easy-to-prepare and delicious meat-free recipes by Bobbie Hinman and Millie Snyder. See order form in back of book.

Each burger provides:			
103	Calories	19 g	Carbohydrate
4 g	Protein	121 mg	Sodium
1 g	Fat	0 mg	Cholesterol

Almost French Fries

French fries without frying? Try them and you'll be amazed at how delicious they can be without any fat at all!

Makes 4 servings

4   medium, baking potatoes, unpeeled, cut into strips
        Salt and pepper to taste

Preheat oven to 450 °.
Lightly oil a large baking sheet or spray with a nonstick cooking spray. Arrange potatoes on prepared sheet in a single layer. Sprinkle with salt and pepper to taste.
Bake 20 to 30 minutes, turning potatoes several times, until desired crispness is reached.

Each serving provides:			
220	Calories	51 g	Carbohydrate
5 g	Protein	16 mg	Sodium
0 g	Fat	0 mg	Cholesterol

Tofu Nuggets

Freezing the tofu makes these nuggets wonderfully chewy on the inside. The wheat germ crust makes them deliciously crisp on the outside. The dipping sauces top it all off!

Makes 4 servings

1   pound firm tofu, frozen and then thawed*, cut into 1-inch cubes
½   cup wheat germ
¼   teaspoon garlic powder (heaping)
⅛   teaspoon pepper
       Salt to taste

Preheat oven to 375 °.
Lightly oil a baking sheet or spray with a nonstick cooking spray.
Place tofu cubes between layers of toweling and gently squeeze out excess water.
In a shallow bowl, combine wheat germ and spices, mixing well.
Fill a small bowl with water.
Dip each piece of tofu first into bowl of water, then shake off excess water and roll in wheat germ. Gently press wheat germ onto tofu with the back of a spoon. Place nuggets on prepared baking sheet.
Bake 25 to 30 minutes, until crisp.
Serve with Dipping Sauces (following).

*Drain tofu slightly, then wrap tightly and place in freezer until solid. Thaw before using.

Each serving provides:			
119	Calories	6 g	Carbohydrate
12 g	Protein	8 mg	Sodium
6 g	Fat	0 mg	Cholesterol

Dipping Sauces

Sweet and Sour Sauce

Also served in the Chinese Restaurant chapter, this sauce is great for dipping.

Makes about ⅓ cup

¼	cup fruit-only peach or apricot jam
½	teaspoon dry mustard
1	teaspoon reduced-sodium (or regular) soy sauce
1	teaspoon white vinegar
1	teaspoon water

In a small bowl or custard cup, combine all ingredients, mixing well. Add more water if a thinner sauce is desired.

Each tablespoon provides:			
42	Calories	12 g	Carbohydrate
0 g	Protein	48 mg	Sodium
0 g	Fat	0 mg	Cholesterol

Maple Mustard

This quick, easy sauce is also great on sandwiches.

Makes about ⅓ cup

¼	cup Dijon mustard
2	tablespoons maple syrup

Combine mustard and maple syrup in a small bowl and mix well.

Each tablespoon provides:			
33	Calories	6 g	Carbohydrate
0 g	Protein	147 mg	Sodium
0 g	Fat	0 mg	Cholesterol

Baked Potato Bar

This is a great meal or snack, either for one or two people or for a crowd. It's easy, it's fun, and it's delicious. For toppings, use your imagination — and your leftovers!

Makes as many servings as desired,
1 medium potato per serving, baked

Toppings: (Choose any or all of the following, or any other low-fat toppings you can think of).

Vegetable toppings:
    Finely chopped onions
    Finely chopped green or red bell peppers
    Steamed chopped broccoli or cauliflower
    Leftover stir-fried vegetables or Chow Mein (see index for recipe)
    Steamed spinach or other greens
Sauces:
    Salsa or picante sauce
    Marinara sauce
    Barbecue sauce
    Nonfat yogurt or soy yogurt
    Bean Gravy (See index for recipe)
    Yogurt-Tahini Sauce (See index for recipe)
Miscellaneous toppings:
    Fresh or dried herbs, such as chives, basil, oregano
    Chopped olives
    Baked beans
    Imitation bacon bits
    Toasted sesame seeds
    Sunflower seeds or pumpkin seeds
    Shredded low-fat Cheddar cheese or soy cheese
    Vegetarian chili (See index for recipe)
    Crumbled Beany Burgers or Sausage (See index for recipes)

To serve, place toppings in bowls. Give each person a baked potato, and be creative!

Each potato provides: (Potato only)			
145	Calories	34 g	Carbohydrate
2 g	Protein	8 mg	Sodium
0 g	Fat	0 mg	Cholesterol

Strawberry Milkshake

Frozen berries make a thick, rich shake. For variations try frozen blueberries or raspberries, or any combination of berries.

Makes 4 servings

2	cups frozen strawberries (unsweetened)
1½	cups cold skim milk or low-fat soymilk
½	cup vanilla or strawberry ice milk or soy-based ice cream
2½	tablespoons sugar or honey
½	teaspoon vanilla extract

Combine all ingredients in a blender container. Blend on high speed until berries are pureéd and mixture is smooth. Add a little more milk if a thinner shake is desired.

Pour into serving glasses and serve right away.

```
                    Each serving provides:

        108   Calories        21   g   Carbohydrate
        4 g   Protein         61  mg   Sodium
        1 g   Fat              4  mg   Cholesterol
```

ITALIAN

Pizza With "The Works" – a tender crust, spread with spicy tomato sauce, then topped with lots of vegetables and your choice of part- skim Mozzarella cheese or soy cheese 34

Stromboli – Italian spiced onions, peppers, and mushrooms, wrapped inside a tender crust and then baked until brown 36

Eggplant Cheese "Steak" – a crusty roll filled with grilled eggplant and piles of steamed onions, then topped with your choice of low-fat Cheddar cheese or soy cheese .. 38

Italian Lentil-Ball Sub – lentil balls, seasoned with Italian spices, smothered with zesty spaghetti sauce, and served on a crusty roll 39

Garlic Bread – slices of tender Italian bread, spread with a mixture of margarine, olive oil, oregano, and fresh garlic, then toasted until crisp 40

Menu

Pizza With "The Works"

You can make this easy pizza at home in less time than it takes to run out and buy one. If you prefer, leave off the cheese and pile on more veggies.

Makes 4 servings

Crust:
¾   cup whole wheat flour
¾   cup all-purpose flour
1   teaspoon baking powder
¼   teaspoon salt
¾   cup plus 1 tablespoon water
Sauce:
1   8-ounce can salt-free (or regular) tomato sauce
¼   teaspoon dried oregano
¼   teaspoon dried basil
⅛   teaspoon garlic powder
Topping:
6   ounces shredded part-skim Mozzarella cheese or soy cheese
       (1½ cups)
¼   cup chopped or thinly sliced onions
1   cup coarsely chopped mushrooms
½   cup chopped green pepper
¼   cup pitted black olives, sliced

Preheat oven to 400 °.
Lightly oil a 12-inch pizza pan, or spray with a nonstick cooking spray.
In a large bowl, combine both types of flour, baking powder, and salt. Mix well. Add water, mixing until all ingredients are moistened. With your hands, work dough into a ball. Place dough in prepared pan. Press in pan to form a crust, flouring your hands slightly to avoid sticking.
Bake 10 minutes. Remove pan from oven.
Combine tomato sauce and spices, mixing well. Spread evenly over baked crust, staying ½-inch away from edge of pan. Sprinkle cheese and then vegetables evenly over sauce.
Bake 10 to 15 minutes, until cheese is melted.

*This recipe is from **Lean and Luscious and Meatless**, a collection of 350 easy-to-prepare and delicious meat-free recipes by Bobbie Hinman and Millie Snyder. See order form in back of book.

Each serving provides:			
318	Calories	43 g	Carbohydrate
17g	Protein	566 mg	Sodium
9 g	Fat	25 mg	Cholesterol

Stromboli

Italian-spiced onions, peppers, and mushrooms wrapped inside a tender crust, makes a scrumptious dinner or snack.

Makes 4 servings

Filling:
2	cups sliced onions
1½	cups sliced green pepper
2	cups sliced mushrooms
3	cloves garlic, finely chopped
1½	teaspoons dried oregano
½	teaspoon dried basil
	Salt and pepper to taste
1	8-ounce can salt-free (or regular) tomato sauce

Crust:
¾	cup whole wheat flour
¾	cup all-purpose flour
1	teaspoon baking powder
⅛	teaspoon salt
2	tablespoons soy margarine
½	cup plus 3 tablespoons skim milk or low-fat soymilk

Heat a large nonstick skillet over medium heat. Add all filling ingredients, except tomato sauce. Add 2 tablespoons of water to skillet, cover, and cook 10 minutes, stirring occasionally. Remove from heat and stir in tomato sauce. Set aside.

In a large bowl, combine both types of flour, baking powder, and salt. Mix well.

Add margarine. Mix with a fork or pastry blender until mixture resembles coarse crumbs.

Add milk, mixing until all ingredients are moistened. With your hands, work dough into a ball. Place on a lightly floured surface and knead a few times. (Add a small amount of flour if dough is sticky.) Roll dough into two 10-inch circles. Place circles on a baking sheet that has been lightly oiled or sprayed with a nonstick cooking spray.

Preheat oven to 400 °.

Spoon half of the filling down the center of each circle o[r]
in about 1-inch of dough at the top and bottom of each circle, the[n]
the sides and tuck the top one underneath, so that filling is com[pletely]
enclosed.

(For a browner crust, using your fingers "paint" the top of the dough
lightly with milk before baking.)

Bake 10 to 15 minutes, until lightly browned.

Each serving provides:			
288	Calories	50 g	Carbohydrate
10 g	Protein	265 mg	Sodium
7 g	Fat	1 mg	Cholesterol

Special
Today =
Stromboli

;gplant Cheese "Steak"

:aks" and piles of steamed onions make this sandwich
) with ketchup or your favorite condiment and dig in!

Makes 4 sandwiches

1	medium eggplant (about 1 pound), peeled and sliced crosswise into ½-inch slices
	Olive oil
	Salt and pepper
	Dried basil
3	cups sliced onions
1	tablespoon reduced-sodium (or regular) soy sauce
2	tablespoons water
1	teaspoon dried basil
4	6-inch sub rolls
4	ounces low-fat Cheddar cheese or soy cheese, sliced or shredded

Preheat broiler or grill. Lightly oil a baking sheet or spray with a nonstick cooking spray.

Place eggplant slices on prepared baking sheet. With your finger, lightly "paint" each slice with olive oil. Sprinkle with salt, pepper, and basil to taste. Turn slices over and repeat on the other side.

Broil or grill eggplant 5 to 7 minutes on each side, or until nicely browned.

While eggplant is cooking, heat a large nonstick skillet over medium-low heat. Add onions, soy sauce, water, and basil. Mix well, breaking onion slices into rings. Cover and cook 10 minutes, or until onions are tender. Stir several times while cooking.

To serve, place eggplant in rolls, slightly overlapping slices. Divide onions and pile on top of eggplant. Top with cheese.

Each serving provides:				
486	Calories	57	g	Carbohydrate
15 g	Protein	1077	mg	Sodium
14 g	Fat	14	mg	Cholesterol

Italian Lentil-Ball Sub

Balls of lentils, rice, and Italian spices on a crusty roll, topped with your favorite spaghetti sauce—Wow!

Makes 6 servings

2	cups cooked lentils (Start with ¾ cup dry lentils and cook in 4 cups of boiling water 45 minutes. Drain well.)
2	cups cooked brown rice
¼	cup very finely minced green pepper
¼	cup very finely minced onions
1	teaspoon dried oregano
½	teaspoon garlic powder
½	teaspoon dried basil
⅛	teaspoon pepper
	Salt to taste
1	32-ounce jar meatless spaghetti sauce (or homemade sauce)
6	6-inch sub rolls

Preheat oven to 375 °.

Lightly oil a baking sheet or spray with a nonstick cooking spray.

In a large bowl, combine lentils, rice, green pepper, onions, and spices. Mix well. Mash well with a fork or potato masher.

Shape mixture into 30 balls about 1¼ inches in diameter and place on prepared baking sheet. With your finger, "paint" each ball lightly with vegetable oil.

Bake 20 minutes.

While lentil balls are baking, place spaghetti sauce in a large saucepan and bring to a boil. Remove from heat and gently place baked lentil balls in sauce.

Cut sub rolls in half lengthwise and open them up, leaving one side attached. Place 5 lentil balls in a row in each roll. (If you wish, you can remove a little of the doughy insides of the rolls to make more room for the lentil balls.) Spoon a little more sauce over balls and close sandwich.

Each serving provides:				
549	Calories	97 g	Carbohydrate
17g	Protein	1426 mg	Sodium
11 g	Fat	0 mg	Cholesterol

Garlic Bread

This delicious, crusty favorite can be enjoyed by itself or served along side any Italian entree.

Makes 8 slices

1	loaf Italian bread
1½	tablespoons soy margarine, softened
1	tablespoon plus 1 teaspoon olive oil
2	cloves garlic, crushed (or ¼ teaspoon garlic powder)
1½	teaspoons dried oregano

Preheat oven to 400 °.

Have a baking sheet ready.

Slice bread into 1-inch slices. Place 8 slices on baking sheet. (Reserve remaining bread for another use.)

In a small bowl or custard cup, combine margarine, olive oil, garlic, and oregano, stirring until mixture is well blended. Spread mixture on top sides of bread, using about ¾ teaspoon on each slice.

Bake 10 to 12 minutes, until crisp. (If a crispier top is desired, place finished bread under the broiler for about a minute, watching carefully to avoid burning.)

Each slice provides:			
95	Calories	12 g	Carbohydrate
2 g	Protein	141 mg	Sodium
4 g	Fat	0 mg	Cholesterol

Egg Rolls – lots of shredded vegetables, lightly stir-fried, then rolled in thin wrappers and browned until crisp 42

Mustard Sauce – a hot and tangy condiment, delicious with all of our dishes 44

Sweet and Sour Sauce – our favorite dipping sauce, made with the finest fruit-only jams 44

Vegetable Chow Mein – a delicious medley of vegetables, lightly steamed and delicately flavored; can be served with strips of crispy stir-fried tofu 45

Vegetable Lo Mein – a delicious combination of vegetables and Oriental noodles, lightly stir-fried in soy sauce 46

Fried Rice – brown rice and vegetables, stir-fried in soy sauce, seasoned with garlic and ginger, and topped with chopped almonds 47

Egg Rolls

Making these Oriental favorites is easier than you think!

Makes 8 egg rolls

2	teaspoons soy sauce
2	tablespoons water
2	teaspoons cornstarch
1	teaspoon each vegetable oil and sesame oil
1½	cups finely shredded cabbage
1½	cups finely shredded Chinese cabbage
½	cup shredded carrots
½	cup canned bamboo shoots, cut into matchstick-size pieces
2	green onions, thinly sliced
1	package egg roll wrappers (Many Oriental grocery stores carry ones that are made without eggs.)
1	teaspoon all-purpose flour
1	tablespoon water

In a small bowl, combine soy sauce, water, and cornstarch. Set aside.

Heat both oils in a large nonstick skillet over medium heat. Add both types of cabbage, carrots, bamboo shoots, and green onions. Cook, stirring, until vegetables are tender, about 3 minutes. Stir soy sauce mixture and drizzle over cabbage mixture. Cook, stirring, 1 minute. Remove skillet from heat.

To assemble, place 2 tablespoons of vegetable mixture diagonally across one wrapper, keeping remaining wrappers covered with a damp towel to prevent drying. Fold bottom corner over filling, then fold over left and right corners. Roll up egg roll to enclose filling. (Most packages of wrappers have handy diagrams to demonstrate the rolling process.) Wrap any remaining wrappers tightly and refrigerate or freeze them for later use.

Combine flour and water in a small bowl or custard cup. With your finger, spread a little on the last corner to seal the edges.

Heat the skillet over medium heat. Oil it lightly or spray with a nonstick cooking spray. With your finger, "paint" a small amount of oil on each egg roll. Place egg rolls in skillet and, turning frequently, cook until brown on all sides. (If you make egg rolls cylindrical, rather than flat, they will brown more evenly.)

Serve with Mustard Sauce or Sweet and Sour Sauce. (Recipes follow).

Each egg roll provides:				
96	Calories	16	g	Carbohydrate
3 g	Protein	74	mg	Sodium
2 g	Fat	0	mg	Cholesterol

Mustard Sauce

Be careful. It's hot! A little goes a very long way!

Makes about 3 tablespoons

2   tablespoons dry mustard
2   tablespoons water

Place mustard in a small bowl or custard cup. Add water, 1 teaspoon at a time, stirring until smooth. Add more water if a thinner sauce is desired.

Each teaspoon provides:			
6	Calories	0 g	Carbohydrate
0 g	Protein	0 mg	Sodium
0 g	Fat	0 mg	Cholesterol

Sweet and Sour Sauce

Slightly sweet and slightly sour, this sauce is great for dipping.

Makes about ⅓ cup

¼   cup fruit-only peach or apricot jam
½   teaspoon dry mustard
1   teaspoon soy sauce
1   teaspoon white vinegar
1   teaspoon water

In a small bowl or custard cup, combine all ingredients, mixing well. Add more water if a thinner sauce is desired.

Each tablespoon provides:			
42	Calories	12 g	Carbohydrate
0 g	Protein	48 mg	Sodium
0 g	Fat	0 mg	Cholesterol

Vegetable Chow Mein

A delicious addition to this tasty dish is strips of tofu, stir-fried until crisp, piled on top of the Chow Mein just before serving.

Makes 4 servings

2	tablespoons reduced-sodium (or regular) soy sauce
⅔	cup water or vegetable broth
2	tablespoons cornstarch
2	teaspoons vegetable oil
1	teaspoon sesame oil
4	cups sliced onions (¼-inch thick)
1	cup sliced celery (¼-inch thick)
⅓	cup carrots, cut into matchstick-size pieces
1	8-ounce can sliced water chestnuts, drained
2	cups bean sprouts
1	cup thinly sliced mushrooms
½	cup snow pea pods, cut diagonally into 1-inch pieces
1	8-ounce can bamboo shoots, drained

In a small bowl, combine soy sauce, water, and cornstarch. Mix to dissolve cornstarch. Set aside.

Heat both types of oil in a large nonstick skillet or wok over medium-high heat. Add onions, celery, carrots, and water chestnuts. Add about 2 tablespoons of water, cover, and cook 5 minutes, stirring occasionally. Add a little more water, if necessary to prevent sticking.

Add bean sprouts, mushrooms, pea pods, and bamboo shoots. Mix well, cover, and cook 3 minutes.

Add soy sauce mixture and cook uncovered, stirring constantly, 1 minute.

Each serving provides:			
198	Calories	36 g	Carbohydrate
6 g	Protein	404 mg	Sodium
4 g	Fat	0 mg	Cholesterol

Vegetable Lo Mein

Add any other vegetables you'd like to this delicious stir-fried favorite.

Makes 4 servings

1	8-ounce package Oriental soba noodles
1	tablespoon vegetable oil
3	tablespoons reduced-sodium (or regular) soy sauce
2	cloves garlic, crushed
1	cup onions, cut into thin slivers
½	cup carrots, cut into matchstick-size pieces
1½	cups sliced mushrooms
½	cup thinly sliced green onions (green part only)
1	cup snow pea pods, cut diagonally into 1-inch pieces

Cook noodles according to package directions. Drain.

Heat 2 teaspoons of the oil and 2 teaspoons of the soy sauce in a large nonstick skillet or wok over medium heat. Add garlic, onions and carrots. Cook, stirring, 3 minutes.

Add mushrooms. Cook, stirring, 3 more minutes. Add green onions, pea pods, cooked noodles, and remaining oil and soy sauce. Cook, stirring, 3 minutes, or until vegetables and noodles are mixed well and heated through.

Each serving provides:			
237	Calories	44 g	Carbohydrate
8 g	Protein	585 mg	Sodium
4 g	Fat	0 mg	Cholesterol

Fried Rice

You can vary the flavors and textures of this favorite Oriental dish by adding different vegetables. For example, try adding fresh or frozen green peas, julienne carrots, or water chestnuts.

Makes 4 servings

2	tablespoons reduced-sodium (or regular) soy sauce
¼	teaspoon garlic powder
¼	teaspoon ground ginger
1	tablespoon vegetable oil
1	teaspoon sesame oil
½	cup chopped onions
½	cup snow pea pods, sliced diagonally into 1-inch pieces
4	cups cold, cooked brown rice
½	cup thinly sliced green onions (green part only)
2	tablespoons chopped almonds

In a small bowl, combine soy sauce, garlic powder, and ginger. Set aside.

Heat both types of oil in a large nonstick skillet or wok over medium-high heat. Add onions and pea pods. Cook, stirring, 2 minutes. Add rice, green onions, and soy sauce mixture. Cook, stirring, 2 to 3 minutes, or until rice is hot.

Spoon into a serving bowl and sprinkle with chopped almonds.

Variations: Add other vegetables of your choice, or small cubes of tofu, along with the onions and pea pods.

Each serving provides:			
288	Calories	49 g	Carbohydrate
7 g	Protein	362 mg	Sodium
8 g	Fat	0 mg	Cholesterol

T.L.T. – thin strips of tofu, cooked until crisp and served on whole wheat toast with lettuce, tomato, and your choice of reduced-calorie or soy mayonnaise 50

Veggie Reuben – shredded cabbage with thinly sliced onions and sweet red peppers, cooked until tender, then grilled between 2 slices of rye bread with our special dressing and your choice of part-skim Mozzarella cheese or soy cheese 51

Potato Knishes – mashed potato patties, with a filled center of crisply browned onions 52

Potato Skins – skins from large baking potatoes, delicately spiced and then baked until crisp 53

Blueberry Tofu Cheesecake – a creamy, rich cheesecake, in a graham cracker crust, topped with sweet, luscious blueberries 54

T.L.T.

This sandwich is quick, easy, and super-delicious. Filled with crisp slices of tofu, it makes a great last minute lunch or dinner.

Makes 2 sandwiches

6   ounces firm tofu, sliced ⅛-inch thick
2   teaspoons reduced-sodium (or regular) soy sauce
4   slices whole wheat bread, toasted
    Lettuce
    Sliced tomato
    Reduced-calorie mayonnaise or soy mayonnaise

Heat a nonstick skillet or griddle over medium heat.

Lightly drizzle soy sauce over tofu slices, using about ⅛ teaspoon on each slice. Place tofu in skillet. Cook, turning several times, until tofu is crisp.

Place tofu on toast with lettuce, tomato, and mayonnaise.

Each sandwich provides:			
212	Calories	27 g	Carbohydrate
13 g	Protein	517 mg	Sodium
8 g	Fat	2 mg	Cholesterol

Veggie Reuben

This veggie version of a popular deli sandwich is chock full of delicious vegetables and flavors.

Makes 2 sandwiches

1½   cups finely shredded cabbage
⅓   cup very thinly sliced onions
⅓   cup sweet red pepper, cut into matchstick-size pieces
1   tablespoon lemon juice
4   slices rye bread
2   ounces part-skim Mozzarella cheese or soy cheese, sliced or
      shredded (½ cup shredded)

Dressing:
2   teaspoons reduced-calorie mayonnaise or soy mayonnaise
2   teaspoons ketchup
1   teaspoon sweet pickle relish
¹⁄₁₆ teaspoon garlic powder
¹⁄₁₆ teaspoon pepper

Lightly oil a large nonstick skillet or spray with a nonstick cooking spray. Heat over medium heat. Add cabbage, onions, red pepper, and lemon juice. Cook, stirring, until vegetables are tender, about 5 minutes. Add small amounts of water, if necessary to prevent sticking.

Divide mixture evenly and pile onto 2 slices of the bread. Divide cheese and place over vegetables.

Combine dressing ingredients in a small bowl or custard cup. Spread dressing on remaining bread slices, then assemble sandwiches.

Reheat skillet over medium heat. Again, oil it lightly or spray with a nonstick cooking spray. Place sandwiches in skillet and cook, turning several times, until both sides are toasted and filling is hot.

Each sandwich provides:			
243	Calories	35 g	Carbohydrate
13 g	Protein	505 mg	Sodium
7 g	Fat	16 mg	Cholesterol

Potato Knishes

Bite into one of these potato patties and taste the surprise onion filling. It's a delicious recipe that can easily be doubled or tripled. The knishes freeze well and can be reheated in a toaster oven or microwave.

Makes 4 knishes

2	cups cooked potatoes, mashed (1½ pounds of potatoes, either baked or boiled, skins removed, will yield about 2 cups of mashed potatoes.)
⅓	cup skim milk or low-fat soymilk
1	tablespoon plus 1 teaspoon vegetable oil
1	tablespoon dried parsley flakes
	Salt and pepper to taste (The knishes are best with *lots* of pepper.)
1	cup chopped onions

In a large bowl, combine mashed potatoes, milk, 1 tablespoon of the oil, parsley, salt, and pepper. Mash well with a fork or potato masher. Add more milk, 1 teaspoon at a time, if potatoes are too dry to hold together.

Heat remaining 1 teaspoon of oil in a large nonstick skillet over medium heat. Add onions and cook, stirring frequently, 5 to 10 minutes, until onions are tender and nicely browned. Remove from heat.

Divide potato mixture evenly into 8 portions and form each one into a 3-inch patty.

Divide onions evenly and place in the center of 4 of the patties. Then top with remaining patties, making 4 thick knishes with the onions sandwiched in the middle. Press edges together to seal.

Reheat the skillet over medium heat. Oil it lightly or spray with a nonstick cooking spray. Place knishes in skillet and cook, turning several times, until nicely browned on both sides.

Each knish provides:			
128	Calories	20 g	Carbohydrate
3 g	Protein	17 mg	Sodium
5 g	Fat	0 mg	Cholesterol

Potato Skins

Instead of the usual fried version, this crispy, crunchy snack is baked. You can make our Potato Knishes or Hash Browns (See index for recipes) and use this recipe for the skins.

Makes 2 servings

2   large baking potatoes, baked (1½ pounds total)
1   teaspoon vegetable oil
       Salt and pepper to taste
       Other spices as desired, such as garlic powder, onion powder,
          dried basil, or dill weed

Preheat oven to 375 °.

Cut each baked potato lengthwise into quarters. With a spoon, scoop out the potato and reserve for another use. Leave a ⅛-inch shell.

Spread oil on inside of potato skins, using ⅛ teaspoon on each skin. Sprinkle with salt and pepper and any other spices of your choice. (For variety, try a different spice on each potato skin.)

Place potato skins on a baking sheet and bake 15 minutes, or until desired crispness is reached.

Serve plain or dip in ketchup or your favorite condiment.

Each serving provides:			
133	Calories	27 g	Carbohydrate
3 g	Protein	12 mg	Sodium
2 g	Fat	0 mg	Cholesterol

Today's Special
— + —
Crispy Potato Skins

Blueberry Tofu Cheesecake

Truly outstanding, this rich, deli-style cheesecake is a real crowd pleaser.

Makes 16 servings

Crust:
¾ cup graham cracker crumbs
2   tablespoons soy margarine, melted
1   tablespoon maple syrup

Filling:
2   pounds soft tofu
1   tablespoon lemon juice
3   tablespoons vegetable oil
½   cup skim milk or low-fat soymilk
1⅓ cups sugar
1   tablespoon all-purpose flour
1   tablespoon plus 1 teaspoon vanilla extract
⅛   teaspoon lemon extract
⅛   teaspoon almond extract

Topping:
2   cups fresh or frozen blueberries (If using frozen berries, there is no
       need to thaw).
2   tablespoons sugar
1   tablespoon plus 1 teaspoon cornstarch
⅔   cup water

Preheat oven to 350 °.

Have a 9-inch spring form pan ready.

In the bottom of the pan, combine graham cracker crumbs, margarine, and maple syrup. Mix well, until crumbs are moistened. Press crumbs firmly into bottom of pan and about ½ inch up the sides.

Bake 8 minutes.

Slice tofu into 1-inch slices and place between layers of toweling. Gently squeeze out excess water. Place half of tofu in a blender container with lemon juice, vegetable oil, half of the milk, and half of the sugar. Blend until smooth. Spoon into a large bowl. Place remaining tofu in blender with the remaining milk, sugar, and other ingredients. Blend until smooth and add to first mixture. Mix well. Pour into prepared crust.

Bake 40 minutes, or until set.

Place blueberries and sugar in a small saucepan. Dissolve cornstarch in water and add to saucepan. Cook over medium heat, stirring frequently, until mixture comes to a boil. Continue to cook, stirring constantly, 1 minute. Remove from heat and let cool 10 minutes, then spoon over cheesecake.

Chill thoroughly.

Each serving provides:				
196	Calories	28	g	Carbohydrate
6 g	Protein	58	mg	Sodium
8 g	Fat	1	mg	Cholesterol

Middle East

Hummus – a creamy spread made from chick peas a.
flavored with garlic and lemon juice; served either as
dip with fresh vegetables, or piled inside a pita bread with
lettuce and tomatoes 58

Tabouleh – a tangy salad of cracked wheat and chopped fresh
vegetables, with a hint of mint; served on a bed of lettuce
and garnished with additional vegetables 59

Baba Ghannouj – garden-fresh eggplant, baked until tender,
then pureéd with garlic and fresh lemon juice; served
with pita triangles for dipping 60

Falafel – spicy little chick pea patties, cooked until golden
brown, piled into a pita bread and topped with lettuce
and tomato and our special Yogurt-Tahini Sauce 61

Yogurt-Tahini Sauce – our special tart and creamy sauce,
made with tahini, lemon juice, and your choice of either
nonfat yogurt or soy yogurt 62

Hummus

*...h lots of lemon and garlic make this creamy spread
...ght. It's delicious piled into a pita bread and topped
...es, or it can be used as a dip for fresh vegetables.*

*Makes 6 servings
(⅓ cup each serving)*

1	19-ounce can chick peas, rinsed and drained (or 2 cups of cooked chick peas)
3	tablespoons lemon juice
¼	cup water
3	cloves garlic, crushed
¼	teaspoon salt
	Dash pepper
3	tablespoons tahini
1	tablespoon finely chopped fresh parsley
	Paprika

In a blender container, combine chick peas, lemon juice, water, garlic, salt, and pepper. Blend until smooth.

Spoon into a bowl and add tahini, stirring until smooth. Sprinkle with parsley and a light dusting of paprika.

Cover and chill several hours, or overnight, to blend flavors.

Each serving provides:			
136	Calories	18 g	Carbohydrate
5 g	Protein	99 mg	Sodium
5 g	Fat	0 mg	Cholesterol

SANDWICHES

Tabouleh

For an authentic presentation, serve this tangy cracked wheat ¿
of romaine lettuce, garnished with tomatoes, cucumbers, blac.
lemon wedges.

Makes 8 servings

2	cups water
1	cup cracked wheat (bulgur), uncooked
¼	cup lemon juice, preferably fresh
1	tablespoon plus 1 teaspoon olive oil
1	large tomato, chopped (1 cup)
1	cup chopped green onion
½	cup finely chopped fresh parsley
¼	cup finely chopped fresh mint leaves
¼	teaspoon pepper
	Salt to taste

Bring water to a boil in a small saucepan. Stir in cracked wheat, cover, and remove from heat. Let stand 20 minutes.

Fluff cracked wheat with a fork and place in a large bowl. Add lemon juice and olive oil. Mix well.

Add remaining ingredients. Mix thoroughly. Add additional lemon juice, salt, or pepper if desired.

Chill several hours to blend flavors. Stir before serving.

Each serving provides:				
101	Calories	17	g	Carbohydrate
3 g	Protein	6	mg	Sodium
2 g	Fat	0	mg	Cholesterol

Baba Ghannouj

Cut a pita bread into triangles and use them to scoop this wonderful dip. It's thick and creamy, with the distinctive flavors of garlic and lemon.

Makes 8 servings
(¼ cup each serving)

1	large eggplant (about 1½ pounds)
3½	tablespoons lemon juice, preferably fresh*
¼	cup tahini
3	large cloves garlic, crushed*
1	tablespoon dried parsley flakes
½	teaspoon salt
⅛	teaspoon pepper

Preheat oven to 400 °.

Cut off and discard the stem end of the eggplant. Place eggplant on a baking sheet and bake 1 hour, or until flesh is very soft and skin is slightly shriveled. Remove from oven and cool slightly.

Cut eggplant in half and, using a spoon, scoop the pulp into a large bowl. Discard the skin. Mash the pulp with a fork and add remaining ingredients, mixing well.

Place mixture in a blender container and blend just until mixture is smooth. (Do not let it blend until it becomes "soupy".)

Spoon into a bowl and chill several hours, or overnight, to blend flavors.

*Use more or less lemon juice and garlic, according to taste.

Each serving provides:			
69	Calories	8 g	Carbohydrate
2 g	Protein	143 mg	Sodium
2 g	Fat	0 mg	Cholesterol

Falafel

Usually deep-fried, these spicy little chick pea patties are browned in a nonstick pan, then piled into a pita bread and topped with lettuce, tomato, and a dollop of creamy Yogurt-Tahini Sauce. (Recipe follows.)

Makes 5 servings
(4 patties each serving)

1	19-ounce can chick peas, rinsed and drained (or 2 cups of cooked chick peas)
2	tablespoons whole wheat flour
1	tablespoon vegetable oil
½	teaspoon garlic powder
½	teaspoon ground cumin
½	teaspoon ground coriander
⅛	teaspoon cayenne pepper
⅛	teaspoon salt

Place chick peas in a large bowl and mash with a fork or potato masher. Add flour and oil and mix well. Sprinkle spices evenly over chick peas and mix well.

Form mixture into balls, about 1¼ inches in diameter, then flatten the balls slightly to form patties. (If mixture is a little dry, add water, 1 teaspoon at a time, until moist enough to hold together.)

Preheat a nonstick griddle or skillet over medium heat. Oil it lightly or spray with a nonstick cooking spray. Place patties on griddle and cook until brown and crisp, turning patties several times and adding a little more cooking spray as needed.

Pile into pita breads while still hot. Add lettuce and tomatoes, or your choice of toppings, and a dollop of Yogurt-Tahini Sauce (see recipe).

Each serving provides:			
141	Calories	20 g	Carbohydrate
5 g	Protein	58 mg	Sodium
4 g	Fat	0 mg	Cholesterol

Yogurt-Tahini Sauce

This tart 'n creamy sauce also makes a great topping for baked potatoes or anything else that is normally topped with sour cream.

Makes about ¾ cup

¼   cup tahini
2   tablespoons lemon juice
¼   teaspoon garlic powder
½   cup plain nonfat yogurt or soy yogurt

Place tahini in a small bowl. Add lemon juice and garlic powder. Sti: until well blended.
Add the yogurt, half at a time, stirring until mixture is smooth.
Chill several hours to blend flavors.
Spoon into Falafel sandwiches.

Each tablespoon provides:		
33 Calories	2 g	Carbohydrate
1 g Protein	5 mg	Sodium
2 g Fat	0 mg	Cholesterol

Cinnamon Buns – delicious buns, rolled with cinnamon, raisins, and brown sugar, and drizzled with icing; served piping hot 64

Carob Chip Brownies – moist, rich brownies, sweetened with molasses and topped with sweet carob chips 66

Dutch Apple Muffins – moist, whole grain muffins with a streusel topping, delicate spices, and lots of chopped fresh apples 67

Toll House Muffins – tender muffins, sweetened with brown sugar and applesauce and loaded with sweet carob chips 68

Blueberry Oat Bran Muffins – our popular high-fiber muffins with lots of blueberries and just a hint of lemon ... 69

Carob Chip Cookies – delectable cookies, flavored with brown sugar and vanilla, and loaded with sweet carob chips 70

menu

Cinnamon Buns

For a real treat, serve these delectable buns piping hot. You won't believe how delicious they are...or how easy!

Makes 10 buns

Topping:
1   tablespoon soy margarine, melted
3   tablespoons maple syrup
2   tablespoons firmly packed brown sugar
2   tablespoons raisins
     Ground cinnamon

Filling:
1   tablespoon firmly-packed brown sugar
½   teaspoon ground cinnamon
2   tablespoons raisins

Dough:
¾   cup whole wheat flour
¾   cup all-purpose flour
1   tablespoon baking powder
1   tablespoon firmly packed brown sugar
3   tablespoons vegetable oil
½   cup orange juice
1   teaspoon vanilla extract

Glaze: (Optional)
¼   cup confectioners sugar
1½   teaspoons skim milk or low-fat soymilk

Preheat oven to 375 °.
Have a 9-inch pie pan ready.
To prepare topping:
Combine melted margarine, maple syrup, and brown sugar in pie pan. Mix well and spread evenly in pan. Sprinkle evenly with raisins and cinnamon. Set aside.
To prepare filling:
Mix together the brown sugar and cinnamon. Set aside, along with the raisins.
To prepare dough:
In a large bowl, combine both types of flour, baking powder, and brown sugar, mixing well. Add oil. Mix with a fork or pastry blender until mixture resembles coarse crumbs. Combine orange juice and vanilla and

add to dough. Mix until all ingredients are moistened. With your hands, work the dough into a ball.

Place dough on a lightly floured surface and knead a few times. Shape dough into a log. Place a piece of wax paper over the dough and roll into an 8 x 16-inch rectangle. Carefully remove wax paper.

Sprinkle dough evenly with filling and raisins.

Starting with one long side, roll dough up tightly like a jelly roll. Cut dough into 10 pieces, using a sharp knife and a sawing motion. (This will keep buns from becoming flattened). Place buns, cut side up, evenly in pan, leaving about ½ inch between buns. With the palm of your hand, press buns down gently until they are touching each other.

Bake 15 minutes.

Let stand 2 to 3 minutes. Then invert onto a serving plate.

To prepare glaze:

Place confectioners sugar in a small bowl or custard cup. Add milk and mix well. (If a thinner glaze is desired, slowly add more milk, a few drops at a time.)

Drizzle glaze over buns and serve right away. (If buns are to be served later, let them cool before glazing.

Each bun (unglazed) provides:			
164	Calories	27 g	Carbohydrate
2 g	Protein	133 mg	Sodium
6 g	Fat	0 mg	Cholesterol

Carob Chip Brownies

These tender, moist brownies have a wonderful texture and a deep carob flavor. Enjoy them plain or, for a very special treat, top a brownie with a Hot Carob-Fudge Sundae (See index for recipe) and you have a Hot Fudge Brownie Delight!

Makes 16 brownies

1½	cups whole wheat flour
⅓	cup carob powder
1	teaspoon baking powder
1	teaspoon baking soda
½	cup applesauce (unsweetened)
½	cup molasses
⅔	cup skim milk or low-fat soymilk
3	ounces tofu, sliced and drained between layers of toweling
1	tablespoon vegetable oil
1	tablespoon vanilla extract
¼	teaspoon almond extract
2	tablespoons carob chips

Preheat oven to 350°.

Lightly oil an 8-inch square baking pan or spray with a nonstick cooking spray.

In a large bowl, combine flour, carob powder, baking powder, and baking soda. Mix well.

In a blender container, combine remaining ingredients, except carob chips. Blend until smooth. Add to dry mixture, mixing until all ingredients are moistened. Place in prepared pan.

Sprinkle carob chips evenly over brownies. Press them down gently into the brownies.

Bake 30 minutes, until a toothpick inserted in the center of the brownies comes out clean.

Cool in pan on a wire rack. Cut into squares to serve.

Variation: Add a few chopped nuts to the batter or to the top of the brownies.

Each brownie provides:				
92	Calories	18	g	Carbohydrate
2	g Protein	105	mg	Sodium
2	g Fat	0	mg	Cholesterol

Dutch Apple Muffins

You'll see why muffins have become so popular when you bite into one of these tender, moist, apple-filled delights.

Makes 9 muffins

Topping:
1½   teaspoons wheat germ
1½   teaspoons firmly packed brown sugar
¼   teaspoon ground cinnamon
Muffins:
1½   cups whole wheat flour
1   teaspoon baking powder
1   teaspoon baking soda
1½   teaspoons ground cinnamon
¼   teaspoon ground nutmeg
⅛   teaspoon ground allspice
1   cup applesauce (unsweetened)
3   ounces tofu, sliced and drained between layers of toweling
2   tablespoons vegetable oil
2   tablespoons skim milk or low-fat soymilk
¼   cup molasses
1½   teaspoons vanilla extract
1   large, sweet apple, unpeeled, cut into ¼-inch pieces (1 cup)

Preheat oven to 400 °.

Lightly oil 9 muffin cups (2½-inch cups) or spray with a nonstick cooking spray.

Combine topping ingredients in a small bowl or custard cup, mixing well. Set aside. In a large bowl, combine flour, baking powder, baking soda, and spices. Mix well.

In a blender container, combine remaining ingredients, except apple. Blend until smooth. Add to dry mixture, along with apple, mixing just until all ingredients are moistened. Divide mixture evenly into prepared muffin cups. Sprinkle with topping.

Bake 15 to 18 minutes, until a toothpick inserted in the center of a muffin comes out clean. Remove muffins to a rack to cool.

Each muffin provides:			
153	Calories	28 g	Carbohydrate
4 g	Protein	176 mg	Sodium
4 g	Fat	0 mg	Cholesterol

Toll House Muffins

The wonderful, sweet flavors of brown sugar and carob chips make these muffins a real taste-tempting treat. Why not pop one in a lunch box in place of a cupcake?

Makes 9 muffins

¾	cup whole wheat flour
¾	cup all-purpose flour
1	teaspoon baking powder
½	teaspoon baking soda
¼	cup carob chips
1	cup applesauce (unsweetened)
3	ounces tofu, sliced and drained between layers of toweling
⅓	cup firmly packed brown sugar
2	tablespoons skim milk or low-fat soymilk
1	tablespoon vanilla extract
1	tablespoon vegetable oil

Preheat oven to 400°.

Lightly oil 9 muffin cups (2½-inch cups) or spray with a nonstick cooking spray.

In a large bowl, combine both flours, baking powder, and baking soda. Mix well. Stir in carob chips.

In a blender container, combine remaining ingredients. Blend until smooth. Add to dry mixture, mixing just until all ingredients are moistened.

Divide mixture evenly into prepared muffin cups.

Bake 15 minutes, until a toothpick inserted in the center of a muffin comes out clean.

Remove muffins to a rack to cool.

Each muffin provides:			
158	Calories	29 g	Carbohydrate
3 g	Protein	112 mg	Sodium
4 g	Fat	0 mg	Cholesterol

Blueberry Oat Bran Muffins

Lots of blueberries provide bursts of flavor in these high-fiber treats. Like most muffins, they are at their best when served warm, just out of the oven.

Makes 9 muffins

1	cup whole wheat flour
1	cup oat bran (uncooked)
1½	teaspoons baking powder
1	teaspoon baking soda
1	teaspoon ground cinnamon
3	ounces tofu, sliced and drained between layers of toweling
1	cup skim milk or low-fat soymilk
¼	cup firmly packed brown sugar
2	tablespoons vegetable oil
1½	teaspoons vanilla extract
¼	teaspoon lemon extract
1	cup fresh or frozen blueberries (If using frozen berries, there is no need to thaw).

Preheat oven to 400 °.

Lightly oil 9 muffin cups (2½-inch cups) or spray with a nonstick cooking spray.

In a large bowl, combine flour, oat bran, baking powder, baking soda, and cinnamon. Mix well.

In a blender container, combine remaining ingredients, except blueberries. Blend until smooth. Add to dry mixture, along with blueberries, mixing until all ingredients are moistened.

Divide mixture evenly into prepared muffin cups.

Bake 18 minutes, until a toothpick inserted in the center of a muffin comes out clean.

Remove muffins to a rack to cool.

Each muffin provides:

169	Calories	26 g	Carbohydrate
6 g	Protein	209 mg	Sodium
5 g	Fat	0 mg	Cholesterol

Carob Chip Cookies

If you prefer moist, chewy cookies, be sure to serve these delicious morsels while they're still warm. What a perfect dessert, snack, or lunch box treat!

Makes 2 dozen cookies

¾ cup whole wheat flour
½ cup all-purpose flour
1 teaspoon baking powder
¼ cup carob chips
½ cup firmly packed brown sugar
3 tablespoons soy margarine, melted
¼ cup orange juice
1 teaspoon vanilla extract

Preheat oven to 375 °.

Lightly oil a baking sheet or spray with a nonstick cooking spray.

In a large bowl, combine both types of flour and baking powder. Mix well. Add carob chips.

In a small bowl, combine remaining ingredients, mixing well. Add to dry mixture, mixing until all ingredients are moistened. Shape dough into 24 balls, using a heaping teaspoonful of dough for each ball. Place on prepared baking sheet, about 2 inches apart.

Place a sheet of wax paper over cookies and flatten them to ½ inch thick, using the bottom of a glass. Carefully remove wax paper.

Bake 12 to 15 minutes, until bottoms of cookies begin to brown.

Remove cookies to a wire rack to cool.

Serve warm or cool completely and store in a container with a loosely fitting lid.

Each cookie provides:				
61	Calories	10	g	Carbohydrate
1 g	Protein	34	mg	Sodium
2 g	Fat	0	mg	Cholesterol

Banana Soft Serve "Ice Cream" – sweet, ripe bananas, frozen and then blended with soft tofu into a creamy ice cream-like dessert 72

Hot Carob-Fudge Sundae – a rich, hot, fudgy sauce spooned over your choice of vanilla ice milk or soy-based ice cream
.... 73

Berry Sweet Smoothie – an icy cold beverage blended from frozen fruits and honey in an orange juice base 74

Malted Milkshake – a thick, rich shake flavored with carob and molasses and blended with your choice of vanilla ice milk or soy-based ice cream 75

Menu

Banana Soft Serve "Ice Cream"

Tofu blended with frozen bananas makes a wonderfully smooth and creamy dessert. It tastes as rich as ice cream and as smooth as frozen custard.

Makes 2 servings

2   medium, ripe bananas
5   ounces soft tofu (about ½ cup)
1   tablespoon sugar
1   teaspoon vanilla extract

Slice bananas crosswise into ¼-inch slices and place on a plate lined with wax paper. Cover and place in the freezer until bananas are frozen.

Slice tofu into 1-inch slices and place between layers of toweling. Gently squeeze out excess water.

Place tofu and frozen bananas in a food processor fitted with a steel blade. Sprinkle with sugar and vanilla. Process just until mixture is smooth.

Divide into 2 serving bowls and serve right away.

(For a special treat, sprinkle with a few carob chips or chopped nuts, or top with strawberry jam before serving.)

Each serving provides:				
187	Calories	35	g	Carbohydrate
7 g	Protein	6	mg	Sodium
4 g	Fat	0	mg	Cholesterol

Hot Carob-Fudge Sundae

A rich, delicious, hot, fudgy sauce spooned over ice milk or soy-based ice cream makes a truly scrumptious dessert.

Makes 4 servings
(2 tablespoons of sauce each serving)

3	tablespoons carob powder
1½	teaspoons cornstarch
½	cup skim milk or low-fat soymilk
3	tablespoons honey or maple syrup
½	teaspoon vanilla extract
	Vanilla ice milk or soy-based ice cream

In a small saucepan, combine carob powder and cornstarch, mixing well. Add about 2 tablespoons of the milk and stir until mixture is very smooth. Gradually add remaining milk, 1 tablespoon at a time, mixing well after each addition. Stir in honey or maple syrup.

Bring mixture to a boil over medium-low heat, stirring constantly. Continue to cook, stirring, 1 minute.

Remove from heat and stir in vanilla extract.

Spoon ice milk or ice cream into serving bowls and top with hot sauce.

Each serving (of sauce only) provides:			
72	Calories	20 g	Carbohydrate
1 g	Protein	17 mg	Sodium
0 g	Fat	1 mg	Cholesterol

Berry Sweet Smoothie

You can change the flavor of this thick, refreshing drink by varying the fruits. Simply freeze the fruits and then blend them. Try strawberries and pineapple, raspberries and bananas, bananas and pineapple.....

Makes 2 servings

1	cup frozen strawberries
½	cup frozen blueberries
1	cup orange juice
½	teaspoon vanilla extract
1	teaspoon honey or sugar

In a blender container, combine all ingredients. Blend until smooth. Add more orange juice if a thinner consistency is desired.

Serve right away.

Each serving provides:				
113	Calories	28	g	Carbohydrate
2 g	Protein	4	mg	Sodium
0 g	Fat	0	mg	Cholesterol

74

Malted Milkshake

Thick and frosty, this rich shake has always been an ice cream parlor favorite. In this one, the combined flavors of carob and molasses really simulate the taste of the calorie-laden original.

Makes 4 servings

1½	cups skim milk or low-fat soymilk
1	tablespoon molasses
1	tablespoon plus 1 teaspoon carob powder
1	teaspoon vanilla extract
1	cup small ice cubes (about 10 small cubes)
½	cup vanilla ice milk or soy-based ice cream

Combine all ingredients in a blender container. Blend on high speed until ice is completely dissolved.

Pour into serving glasses and serve right away.

Each serving provides:				
74	Calories	13	g	Carbohydrate
4 g	Protein	63	mg	Sodium
1 g	Fat	4	mg	Cholesterol

Index

SHARE THE DELIGHTS OF
HEALTHFUL COOKING WITH A FRIEND

Dear Bobbie,

I'd like to order copies of the following titles:

_____copies of *Burgers 'n Fries 'n Cinnamon Buns*
at $6.95 each for a total of   _____
Postage and handling – $1.50 for each book   _____

_____copies of *Lean and Luscious and Meatless*
at $15.95 each for a total of   _____
Postage and handling – $2.50 for each book   _____

                              Subtotal   _____
                              Total   _____

Check or money order enclosed for $_____

Ship to:

Name_____

Address_____

City_____State_____Zip_____

Make checks payable to:

BOBBIE E. HINMAN
P.O. BOX 8100
NEWARK, DE 19714-8100

Notes

Notes

Ask your store to carry our fine line of vegetarian cookbooks
or you may order directly from

Book Publishing Company:

American Harvest.....$11.95
Burgers 'n Fries 'n Cinnamon Bins.....$6.95
Cooking with Gluten and Seitan.....$7.95
Cookin' Healthy with One Foot Out the Door.....$8.95
Ecological Cooking.....$10.95
From A Traditional Greek Kitchen.....$9.95
George Bernard Shaw Vegetarian Cookbook.....$8.95
Healthy Cook's Kitchen Companion.....$12.95
Instead of Chicken, Instead of Turkey.....$9.95
Judy Brown's Guide to Natural Foods Cooking.....$10.95
Kids Can Cook.....$9.95
Murrieta Hot Springs Vegetarian Cookbook.....$9.95
New Farm Vegetarian Cookbook.....$7.95
Now and Zen Epicure.....$17.95
The Peaceful Cook.....$8.95
The Shiitake Way.....$7.95
The Shoshoni Cookbook.....$12.95
Simply Heavenly.....$19.95
Soups for All Season.....$9.95
The Sprout Garden.....$8.95
Starting Over: Learning to Cook with Natural Foods.....$10.95
Tempeh Cookbook.....$10.95
Ten Talents.....$18.95
Tofu Cookery, revised.....$14.95
Tofu Quick & Easy.....$7.95
TVP Cookbook $6.95
The Uncheese Cookbook.....$11.95
Uprisings: The Whole Grain Bakers' Book....$13.95
Vegetarian Cooking for Diabetics.....$10.95
Nutrition and Health:
A Physician's Slimming Guide.....$5.95
Power of Your Plate.....$10.95

To order, please include $2 *per book* for postage and handling.
Mail your order to:
Book Publishing Company
P.O. Box 99
Summertown, TN 38483

Or call: **1-800-695-2241**